Let's Look at Animals

by Emma Rattenbury

SCHOOL PUBLISHERS

Cover ©Alamy; 2 (t), (c) ©Alamy; 2 (b) ©Auscape International Photo Library; 3, 4 ©Alamy; 5 ©Photolibrary.com; 6 ©Alamy; 7 ©Auscape International Photo Library; 8 ©Photolibrary.com.

Printed in the United States of America

ISBN 10: 0-15-350391-2
ISBN 13: 978-0-15-350391-7

Ordering Options
ISBN 10: 0-15-350331-9 (Grade 1 Below-Level Collection)
ISBN 13: 978-0-15-350331-3 (Grade 1 Below-Level Collection)
ISBN 10: 0-15-357416-X (package of 5)
ISBN 13: 978-0-15-357416-0 (package of 5)

2 3 4 5 6 7 8 9 10   179   15 14 13 12 11 10 09 08 07

There are many kinds
of animals. Each has ways
that help it live.

This animal has soft
feet and toes. How does
this help?

Soft feet help this
animal catch other animals
to eat. The other animals
can't hear it coming.

This animal uses its legs to leap high. How does this help?

Leaping helps the animal see farther. It may see other animals that only want to catch it. Then it can run away.

These animals have hair. It is the color of where they live.

This animal has clear
scales over its eyes. How
does this help?

The scales keep out
dust. This animal likes to
sit in the warm sun.
Good-bye, animals!